THE KREMLIN COUP

Laurie Nadel

THE MILLBROOK PRESS
Brookfield, Connecticut

Published by The Millbrook Press
2 Old New Milford Road
Brookfield, CT 06804
© 1992 Blackbirch Graphics, Inc.
First Edition

Created and produced in association with Blackbirch Graphics.
Series Editor: Bruce S. Glassman

Library of Congress Cataloging-in-Publication Data
Nadel, Laurie.
    The Kremlin coup/Laurie Nadel.
    Includes bibliographical references and index.
    Summary: Describes the August 1991 coup attempt that resulted in the
collapse of communism in the Soviet Union.
    1. Soviet Union—History—Coup d'état, 1991—Juvenile literature. [1.
Soviet Union—History—Coup d'état, 1991.] I. Title. II. Series.
ISBN 1-56294-170-4   91-36892
DK292.N33 1992   CIP
947.085'4—dc20   AC

Acknowledgments and photo credits

Cover, pp. 22, 30, 31, 49, 58: Wide World Photos; pp. 4, 7 (left), 23:
©Novosti/Gamma-Liaison; pp. 6 (left), 7 (middle), 7 (right), 15, 17, 20, 26,
43: Gamma-Liaison; pp. 6 (middle), 9, 10: ©Boris Yurchenko/Wide World
Photos; p. 6 (right): ©Palumbo/Gamma-Liaison; pp. 14, 35: ©Alexander
Zamlianichenko/Wide World Photos; p. 21: ©Art Zamur/Gamma-Liaison;
p. 25: ©Czarek Sokolowski/Wide World Photos; p. 28: ©Alik Keplicz/Wide
World Photos; p. 33: ©Sergei Karpukhin/Wide World Photos; pp. 36, 40:
©Georges Merillon/Gamma-Liaison; p. 44: ©Dusan Vranic/Wide World
Photos; p. 45: ©Richard Drew/Wide World Photos; p. 50: ©Chip Hires/
Gamma-Liaison; p. 52: ©Vlastimir Shone/Gamma-Liaison; p. 53: ©L. Van Der
Stockt/Gamma-Liaison; p. 54: ©Liu Heung Shing/Wide World Photos; p. 60:
©Stephen Ferry/Gamma-Liaison.
Maps and charts by David Bell.
Special thanks to Cindy Dopkin and Elvis Brathwaite.

Many thanks to Terry Stewart of CBS News and the staff of the
CBS News library, Judy Bavasi, Dorothy Beach, Helen McNeill,
Roy Murphy, Mildred Nadel, and Yoram Rostas. My deepest
appreciation goes to Nancy Quade of the Brooklyn Public
Library whose magical research saved the day (again). Thanks
to Bruce and Richard Glassman for trusting me with this
challenging assignment and for their encouragement.

For Phil and Charly

Contents

Chapter One/ The Coup 5

Chapter Two/ The Fall of Communism 29

Chapter Three/ The Old Order Breaks Down 51

Chapter Four/ New Global Alliances 55

Chapter Five/ Looking Toward the Future 59

Chronology 62

For Further Reading 62

Index 63

Chapter 7

The Coup

Dateline: Moscow. Monday, August 19, 1991, 6 A.M. News bulletin: "Vice President Gennady Yanayev has taken over the duties of president of the USSR, in keeping with Article 127, Clause 7 of the Soviet Constitution due to Mikhail Gorbachev's inability to perform his duties for health reasons."

As Tass, the official Soviet news agency, issues its bulletin, morning rush hour begins in Moscow. Thousands of Muscovites heading to their places of work are wondering if Tass is telling the truth. Is the Soviet leader really sick? Or is this another case of Communist "disinformation," a lie disguised as truth to serve some secret political end? Commuters coming into the city from the west are the first to glimpse the truth when they see a long column of tanks heading for the center of the Soviet capital.

Soviet Vice President Gennady Yanayev and the seven other men taking over the Kremlin are calling themselves the State Committee for the State of Emergency. Yanayev was hand-picked for the vice-presidency by Soviet President Mikhail Gorbachev himself. "I want someone alongside me I can trust," Gorbachev said the year before. Now, the man he trusted has betrayed him.

Several hours after seizing power, the Emergency Committee bans all meetings and political parties, shutting

> Soviet Vice President Gennady Yanayev and seven other men took over the Kremlin

Opposite:
An army tank sits poised in front of St. Basil's Cathedral in Moscow's Red Square. The clocktower at left sits just outside the walls of the Kremlin.

The Coup Plotters
A Who's Who in Betrayal
(Emergency Committee Members)

Yanayev

Vladimir Kryuchkov—The sixty-seven-year-old KGB chief vocally opposed Gorbachev's attempts to repair East-West relations. In December 1990, he gave a television speech warning that the future of the Soviet Union was in doubt and that a crackdown on "radical" elements was going to occur.

Yazov

Kryuchkov

Gennady Yanayev—Mikhail Gorbachev's hand-picked vice president declares himself acting president on Monday, August 19. A career Communist party member (called an *apparatchik*), Yanayev is a conservative who opposes *perestroika* and other economic reforms.

Dmitri Yazov—Prior to the coup, the sixty-seven-year-old defense minister was believed to be loyal to Gorbachev although he opposed the decision to pull troops out of Eastern Europe.

Valentin Pavlov—Reported to be hospitalized for hypertension early on in the coup, Pavlov earns the displeasure of fellow Emergency Committee members for his hesitancy in supporting the coup in its

down independent newspapers that supported Soviet leader Gorbachev's economic reforms, called *perestroika,* and the new freedom, called *glasnost.* (Under past Communist leaders, criticism of the government was forbidden and any freedom of expression was suppressed.) Taking his cue from the other hardliners in the Emergency Committee, Yanayev blames the newspapers for inciting sentiment against the Communist party. *The Moscow News* loses no time defying the regime, transmitting news stories via fax machine. The Emergency Committee also orders Soviet troops to shut down independent Radio Russia and Russian television, both outspoken voices for reform and both critical of the Communist party. Television and radio station employees arrive at their offices to find the way blocked by soldiers.

Pavlov

early stages. He is dismissed as prime minister. Prior to holding his post, he was a public finance bureaucrat who was considered unsuccessful in dealing with the growing budget deficit.

Aleksandr Tizyakov—Little is known about this man, the head of the industrialists' union, a vast umbrella association that controls construction, transport, and communications enterprises as well as industrial production. It is speculated that he joined the coup plotters because of dissatisfaction with his career.

He is reported to have a drinking problem.

Oleg Baklanov—The Soviet Communist party secretary is a shadowy figure who wielded control over the Soviet defense industry. In recent years, with Communist party

Baklanov

power waning, Baklanov has seen his own influence over the military-industrial complex falling, and he was reportedly being edged out of power.

Vasil Starodubsev—Chairman of the Soviet farmers' union, Starodubsev holds strongly conser-

vative views on farming. He supported the old collective farming system and opposed reform proposals that would give land and greater independence to Soviet farmers.

Boris Pugo—Appointed interior minister to replace liberal Oleg Bakatin, Boris Pugo, fifty-three, headed the Latvian KGB. He was considered responsible for the crackdown against Latvian nationalists that started early in 1991. (Pugo committed suicide after shooting and injuring his wife when pro-Gorbachev police came to arrest him for his role in the coup.)

Pugo

With growing anxiety, people around the world turn on their televisions for news. In Moscow, it is clear that something is wrong when viewers tune into a morning concert. "My mother told me there was trouble," one thirteen-year-old girl would later recall. "Soviet television was playing light classical music early in the morning. They never play such good music unless something is wrong."

As news of the Kremlin coup spreads, so does concern over the fate of Soviet President Mikhail Gorbachev. Considered one of the most important political leaders of the twentieth century, Gorbachev, winner of the 1990 Nobel Peace Prize, seems to have simply "disappeared." With Gorbachev gone, another frightening question comes to mind: Who now controls the Soviet Union's huge nuclear arsenal?

Monday, August 19, 1991

It is now mid-morning in Moscow, several hours after the first tanks have moved into the streets. While the Emergency Committee plans its next step inside the Kremlin building, people begin gathering in the streets.

Not far from the Kremlin, in the Russian Parliament building (nicknamed the Russian White House because of its color), Russian Federation President Boris Yeltsin is meeting with his advisers. Yeltsin is the president of Russia, the largest of the fifteen Soviet republics. The first elected leader in Russian history, Yeltsin is especially popular with the people because he has given up his membership in the Communist party after a dispute with his former friend and political ally Mikhail Gorbachev. Yeltsin's open criticism of corruption among Communist party officials has angered the Soviet president, who also serves as general secretary of the Communist party. Although Gorbachev and Yeltsin believe that political and economic change is necessary, Gorbachev still has an allegiance to the party while Yeltsin has broken away and is considered by the Soviet establishment—and by President George Bush—to be a political "maverick," or loner.

Boris Yeltsin makes his first move against the Emergency Committee indirectly, dispatching his press secretary into the streets with a message: "We are dealing with an unconstitutional, reactionary coup."

Two hours later, Yeltsin emerges from the Russian Parliament building and climbs on top of a "friendly" armored truck, shaking hands with the astonished soldiers inside. Shouting to the crowd, he speaks about the coup. They "will not triumph," he shouts, calling for a general strike. The deputy mayor of Moscow supports Yeltsin's call for resistance. Black-and-white posters announcing the strikes and demonstrations suddenly appear in the Metro, Moscow's underground train system. The mayor of Leningrad stands behind Yeltsin, as well. In the countryside, Russian coal miners prepare to strike.

Opposite:
A line of tanks rolls through the streets of downtown Moscow early in the morning of August 19, 1991.

The People Protest

Throughout the day, thousands of people flock into the streets, building barricades around the Russian White House where Boris Yeltsin and his advisers are encamped. The protesters, many of them young, drive buses and trolley cars to the parliament square to prevent tanks from getting through. With collective strength, they move tree trunks, bathtubs, and vehicles to form barricades. Some protesters even lie down in front of the approaching tanks, forcing the soldiers to stop. Hundreds of people link arms and form human chains to keep the armed troops from moving into the square.

When the Emergency Committee orders fresh troops into Moscow, the arriving soldiers defect. Instead of moving against the Russian president, the new soldiers line up their tanks to help guard him. From inside the Parliament

As soon as Moscow's citizens learned of the coup, they took to the streets in protest. Hundreds created barricades with buses and trolley cars, locked arms in the streets to prevent troops from moving, and jumped on tanks in an effort to stop the military takeover.

building, Yeltsin is calling for more people to resist the new leaders. When they cut off his telephone, Yeltsin picks up a cellular phone and boldly continues his phone campaign. Although the official Soviet news media do not carry any of this, Yeltsin's appeals for help are broadcast around the world, beamed back into the Soviet Union by the Voice of America and the British network, BBC.

Demonstrations spread through Moscow. When four military trucks start driving in circles in order to frighten a crowd outside a theater, people rush into the street, shouting "Shame! Shame!" at the soldiers. This is not the type of response that the ruling junta expects. In plotting this takeover, the Emergency Committee had counted on the legendary passivity of the people. Russians, in particular, have long suffered under repressive totalitarian regimes. Before the Communists came to power after the Bolshevik revolution in 1917, the Russian czars killed thousands of innocent people in massacres called *pogroms*. Frustrated, self-declared Acting President Gennady Yanayev calls Boris Yeltsin on a special "hot line." When they get on the phone together, the two men shout curses at each other.

Condemnation from the West

In the United States, where he is vacationing in Kennebunkport, Maine, President George Bush is shocked to hear that Mikhail Gorbachev has been overthrown. He calls the coup "a disturbing development which could have serious consequences for U.S.-Soviet relations." (Just a few weeks earlier, on July 31, President Bush and Soviet leader Gorbachev met in Moscow to sign a strategic arms reduction treaty.) Mr. Bush next confers by phone with Polish President Lech Walesa and Czechoslovakian President Vaclav Havel. Both men are leaders in the fight against communism in their respective countries. They urge President Bush to speak against the Emergency Committee's takeover. But the president seems reluctant to anger the new Soviet leaders by issuing a statement.

Pentagon officials, worried about Soviet nuclear codes falling into the wrong hands and concerned about the possibility of a civil war, follow the president's cue by deciding not to officially raise the military alert condition among U.S. forces around the world. However, quiet steps are taken to deploy contingency forces of U.S. Marines in the eastern Mediterranean, the Persian Gulf region, and the western Pacific—just in case.

Later in the day, the United States announces that it will not supply aid to the new government, which it calls "unconstitutional." President Bush joins German Chancellor Helmut Kohl, French President François Mitterrand, and British Prime Minister John Major in a move to stop all future economic aid to the new regime. In a joint statement, the Western leaders say that the Soviet coup is "impossible to justify" and call on the new Soviet rulers to guarantee Mr. Gorbachev's safety.

State of Emergency

At 5 P.M., Gennady Yanayev holds a press conference that is televised worldwide. His hands are shaking as he speaks, which many see as a signal that the Emergency Committee is shaky, too. Yanayev says the committee has acted to prevent "the breakup of the Soviet Union. We have to take resolute action in order to stop the country from sliding down to a disaster." Insisting that the Emergency Committee is "determined to restore law and order," Yanayev announces a state of emergency in Moscow, publicly warning Russian President Boris Yeltsin that any attempts to fight the new government will fail.

While Yanayev's threat sinks in, the big question in many people's minds concerns Soviet leader Gorbachev. When a reporter asks, "Where is he?" there is no doubt that the "he" in question is Gorbachev.

"Mikhail Gorbachev is now on vacation," Yanayev replies. "He's undergoing treatment in the south of our country. He is very tired after these many years and he will need some time to get better. I hope that my friend President Gorbachev will return to his office and we will work together."

Reporters begin to jeer. Hardly anyone believes him.

It is clear to many people watching Yanayev's televised news conference that, while new leaders have taken power, they are not entirely in command.

Gorbachev Under House Arrest

Imprisoned in his luxurious beachfront estate (called a *dacha*) on the coast of the Crimean Sea, Soviet President Gorbachev is listening to the news conference on a make-shift radio that can pick up the Voice of America and the BBC. He is encouraged to hear people booing Gennady Yanayev.

Gorbachev's house arrest began the previous night. At approximately 4:50 P.M., Gorbachev's bodyguard quietly announced that the Soviet president had visitors. Gorbachev said that he was not expecting anyone. When he picked up his telephone to call one of his aides, the line was dead. He tried another telephone, then a third, and a fourth. All communications between the highest official of the Soviet Union and the rest of the world had been disconnected. Gorbachev, his wife Raisa, their daughter, son-in-law, and granddaughter then gathered in the living room. Outside, a group of men were pounding on his door. Gorbachev said, "If the worst happens, I will stand up for my position and will not yield to any blackmail." His family promised to support him, whatever he did.

Soon, the men pushed their way into his house.

"Who sent you?" Gorbachev asked.

"The Committee," they replied.

"Who appointed such a committee? I didn't. The Supreme Soviet didn't." (The Supreme Soviet is the equivalent of the U.S. Congress.)

The men did not answer him. They told Gorbachev to sign a statement supporting them. He refused. Then they

A woman kneels and prays for the people of Russia while protesters climb one of the many tanks that surrounded the Russian Federation building.

told him to give his power to Gennady Yanayev, his trusted vice president. Gorbachev refused again. "You're going to kill yourselves. The hell with you. You'll kill the country as well," Gorbachev said. The men urged him to resign as president.

"You'll never live that long. You are all going to meet defeat," Gorbachev warned as they were leaving.

Gorbachev had been scheduled to return to Moscow in time to sign a new all-union treaty granting greater independence to the fifteen republics under Soviet control. The treaty signing was to take place on Tuesday, August 20.

One of the world's superpowers, the Soviet Union covers one-sixth of the earth's land surface. Its population of 287 million people contains one hundred different nationalities. Increasingly, they have demanded greater independence from Moscow.

Indecisive at first, Gorbachev did not know whether to respect or crush the independence movement. But he finally decided that giving the republics more power would prevent civil war. To accomplish this goal, the proposed new treaty would change the name of the Union of Soviet Socialist Republics to the Union of Soviet Sovereign Republics. Each republic would create its own sovereign, elected government. But many hardliners in the ruling Communist party objected strongly to the treaty. They believe that the central government should continue to wield strong control and are furious at Mikhail Gorbachev. This coup is their attempt to stop him.

Alliances changed quickly during the first days of the coup. Young soldiers who were sent to Moscow in tanks soon had a change of heart. Many troops refused to take action against fellow citizens and switched their allegiance from the coup leaders to Boris Yeltsin.

Tuesday, August 20, 1991

Tuesday seems like another ordinary workday in many districts of Moscow. Lovers stroll in the parks, people go to their jobs, and many seem unaware of the drama unfolding several miles away in the center of town. Judy Bavasi, an American teacher visiting Moscow, tells an interviewer, "People in Moscow don't seem afraid. There is no terror. In fact, many people are buying ice cream from sidewalk vendors. If anything, people are walking around trying to find out what's going on." The official Soviet television station reports that "the people of Moscow have welcomed the troops with kindness." People carrying transistor radios and boom boxes listen for any reports about Gorbachev's health. Most people are suspicious of the official version that he is "too ill to govern." The hardline Communist governments and the state-run media have simply lied for too many years to be credible sources of information for most Soviet citizens. For years, a standard Soviet joke posed the following question: "How do you read *Pravda* (the official Communist party newspaper)?" Answer: "Between the lines."

The new leaders, who expected the Soviet people to obey them out of fear, are witnessing a surprising display of anti-government feeling. The areas around Red Square, the Kremlin, and the Russian Parliament are now surrounded by armored personnel carriers, tanks, and soldiers. Truckloads of riot police are standing by, in the event they are needed. Yet, in defiance of the ban on public gatherings, tens of thousands of protesters have gathered in the center of Moscow, much as the students in China gathered in Tiananmen Square during the "Beijing Spring" of 1989. One protester describes the scene at the center of Moscow as "a sea of remaining democracy." Many students participating in the demonstrations are worried about how the coup will affect their education. "What if the new government closes the schools?" one girl wonders. "Will I have to pick potatoes?" Many teenage boys express concern that

they may be drafted into the military. Some of them wonder aloud, "What will happen if I have to shoot my fellow students?"

Yeltsin's Appeal

Inside the Russian Parliament this morning, Russian Federation President Boris Yeltsin is on the phone with President George Bush, asking for American support. Yeltsin tells Bush that he thinks that he can hold out long enough for the Soviet people to defeat the coup. Previously Bush had been cool toward Yeltsin because the outspoken Russian had criticized Mikhail Gorbachev for not being bold enough. Now, President Bush concedes he is impressed when Yeltsin says, "I think the tanks are coming. I don't have much time."

By Tuesday, August 20, tens of thousands of people had gathered around the Russian Parliament building to defend Boris Yeltsin and to show support for his democratic reforms.

At noon, Boris Yeltsin leaves the building to address the thousands of protesters gathered outside. "The junta used no restraint in grabbing power and the junta feels itself under no constraints to keep it," he says, promising to hold out for as long as it takes to remove the "illegal junta and bring it to justice." He calls on the crowd to demand the ruling committee's "immediate resignation." Many people in the crowd are frightened. Rumors are spreading fast. According to one rumor, Yeltsin is going to be arrested momentarily. Another rumor says that the tanks are coming and that helicopters are about to drop tear gas and fire bullets at the demonstrators. Since the start of Communist rule in the Soviet Union, human rights have been severely repressed. Simply voicing an opinion that is critical of the Communist government has, in the past, meant almost certain arrest, torture, and long years of exile in the icy work camps of Siberia. The Soviet secret police, the dreaded KGB, have infiltrated all ranks of Soviet life, a lurking, sinister presence that monitors any disobedience or disagreement with government policy. With this political heritage, thousands of people are risking their lives this Tuesday by showing their opposition to the coup. They are aware that the consequences could be severe.

At another rally outside City Hall, former foreign minister Eduard Shevardnadze adds his voice to Yeltsin's. (Shevardnadze was one of the first government officials to warn Gorbachev of a possible military dictatorship.) "Long Live Freedom!" he shouts to a cheering crowd.

Coup Leaders Become "Sick"

"In world history, coup attempts generally succeed or fail in the first three days," observes Vladimir Lukin, chairman of the international affairs committee of the Russian Parliament. "If the people who planned the coup in the Soviet Union do not achieve victory very soon, then the attempt could collapse. The situation will become clearer in the next few hours."

Prophetic words. By Tuesday afternoon, several of the eight members of the State Committee for the State of Emergency are reported to have "fallen ill." Aleksandr Bessmertnykh, the foreign minister, is reported sick after returning to Moscow from vacation. One official report says that Bessmertnykh is "expected to return to work in a few days." (Later, it will be said that Bessmertnykh supported the coup but was not an official member of the Emergency Committee.) Defense Minister Dmitri Yazov is suddenly sick with an unnamed illness, as well. He is immediately replaced by General Mikhail Moiseyev. Prime Minister Valentin Pavlov suddenly comes down with unexplained "severe fluctuation of hypertension." KGB Chairman Vladimir Kryuchkov is also sick with a mysterious, sudden illness. Reading between the lines, Boris Yeltsin says that the popular backlash was so strong that the coup leaders realized there was no way they could win. So they have manufactured "illnesses" to save face as they drop out of the ruling committee. ("The big lie," or bending the truth was a hallmark of Joseph Stalin, who ruled the Soviet Union with a tyrannical hand from 1929 until 1953. Millions of innocent Soviet citizens were massacred during Stalin's oppressive and brutal regime.)

The legacy of Stalin is government by intimidation. Hoping that he can establish his authority by acting tough, coup spokesman Gennady Yanayev imposes an 11 P.M. curfew for Moscow residents. "Students are terrified by the curfew," says Judy Bavasi. "The thought of being shot if you get caught after curfew is on everyone's mind." Throughout the afternoon, Russian legislators gather in Boris Yeltsin's office to deliver speeches that are broadcast live on Moscow Radio, which continues to operate in defiance of the government order to stop. Several legislators say they think this is the last time they will speak to the people because tanks are moving in. When British Prime Minister John Major reaches Yeltsin by telephone, the sound of tanks can be heard through the phone line.

Night Vigil

Tuesday night, thousands more men and women risk being shot for violating the curfew as they take up positions outside the Russian Parliament. Even though it is raining, they stand thirty-deep in front of the building, waiting for word of a possible military attack on the building. Many of them wear tricolor Russian flags as armbands or headbands to show their support for Boris Yeltsin. One young woman who holds a sign reading "Soldiers! Don't Shoot Your People" comments, "Tonight marks the end of my life of endless passivity." If necessary, she says she is ready to die resisting the pending attack.

The mood in the crowd is tense. Will the soldiers gun them down or will they, too, defect to Yeltsin's side? It is hard to know. The Soviet Army is made up of more than 3,500,000 troops from all parts of the USSR. It is unclear whether their loyalties are to Gorbachev or their immediate commanders. Nor does anyone know whether the soldiers will fire on their own people when the test comes tonight. Technically, the troops are under the command of the Communist party, which is ruled by General Secretary Mikhail Gorbachev. Defense Minister Yazov has often said that no Soviet troops will fire on Soviet people. But many senior military officers are fed up with Gorbachev. His attempts at *perestroika*, changing the economy from a centrally controlled, state-run system to a free market, have not reduced the chronic shortages of food and other supplies, as had been hoped. Low pay for the troops and housing shortages are creating additional hardships for soldiers returning home to the Soviet Union from duty stations abroad. Many soldiers are deserting the Soviet Army in Germany. Military leaders are also upset with Gorbachev because of his 1989 decision to withdraw from Afghanistan, which the Soviets had invaded and occupied in December 1979. They are angry, too, because Gorbachev is pulling Soviet troops from Eastern Europe

A photograph of Russian President Boris Yeltsin is held high above the crowd assembled outside the Russian "White House."

and because he has signed an agreement with the United States to reduce nuclear weapons stockpiles.

The first shots are fired just after midnight. The crowds of civilians defending the Russian Parliament begin to shout, "Shame! Shame! Russia! Russia!" Flares and tracer bullets light up the sky after a group of armored cars gets caught in a tunnel near the Kremlin. Other tanks are stopped at the makeshift barricades built by the thousands of demonstrators.

Inside the Russian Parliament building, the mood is somber. Boris Yeltsin has set up a war room where young politicians, scholars, journalists, and military experts help coordinate the resistance effort. After eating food bused in from the Moscow McDonald's, Yeltsin walks through the halls, waiting to find out if he is going to be taken captive or killed. Fresh rumors say that the troops will storm the building in half an hour, then ten minutes. But there is no showdown.

At 2:30 A.M., Yeltsin learns that Gennady Yanayev has promised not to attack the Russian Parliament. There is a moment of relief followed by uncertainty. Who can be sure that Yanayev can be trusted? After all, Mikhail Gorbachev had trusted him, only to be betrayed.

Several hours later, a column of nine armored vehicles approaches the Russian White House. According to *The Washington Post*, a young man tries to throw a cloth over the peephole of one of the military trucks. When its gun swings around, the young man is knocked to the ground and crushed beneath the wheels. People in the crowd drop flowers into small pools formed by the rain mixed with blood. Automatic rifle fire is heard somewhere in the crowd. Protesters respond by throwing Molotov cocktails at the armored cars. Two other young men are reported killed in the melee. By morning, the official count is three dead and four wounded.

Shortly before dawn, a Jeep pulls up to the crowd. When an officer gets out, he is asked whether he supports Boris

Protesters constructed high barricades around the Russian Parliament building. Their fortress was made of everything from bathtubs to wooden desks to mattresses and box springs.

By Wednesday, August 21, protesters were tired and edgy. Here, two anti-coup demostrators scuffle over whether to allow an armored personnel carrier to pass through the area.

Yeltsin or the Emergency Committee. The officer waves his arms in frustration, "Who knows who the hell I am with?" By daylight the column of armored vehicles also defects, joining with the resistance.

Wednesday, August 21, 1991

By 10 A.M., the State Committee for the State of Emergency is ready to give up. The leaders of the coup start by blaming one another for the failure. Prime Minister Pavlov blames Acting President Gennady Yanayev for giving him inaccurate information about Gorbachev's health. Yanayev, in turn, shifts the blame to other members of the Committee. "They are all too frightened to take responsibility for their actions," one of Boris Yeltsin's foreign policy advisers observes. "There were soldiers who would have carried out an order to shoot, but nobody was willing to take the terrible responsibility of issuing such an order. This was not China or even Chile, where a Pinochet was willing to take responsibility on himself. You can't organize a coup by committee."

Inside the Russian Parliament, Russian legislators (called deputies) stand up to honor the three demonstrators who were killed. The mood in the Parliament chamber is angry and defiant at first, but everyone in the chamber starts cheering when Yeltsin announces that all eight members of the Emergency Committee are heading for the airport to get out of town. When Yeltsin proposes that Parliament adopt a resolution calling for the immediate arrest of the eight Committee members, the Russian Parliament votes without delay. Deputy Chairman Ivan Laptev announces the parliamentary decision on television, explaining that a commission will investigate the Emergency Committee's crimes and bring them to trial. Yeltsin begins a purge of all officials in Russia who supported the coup.

By mid-afternoon, some of Gorbachev's aides, silent for the past three days, begin holding press conferences to say that they have been against the coup all along. Adding their voices to the disclaimers are Soviet Communist party leaders who insist that they are opposed to "attempts to establish an authoritarian regime." They call for Mikhail Gorbachev's release.

Troops and Tanks Depart

Outside, in the streets, the military convoys begin pulling out of Moscow. A three-mile column of 180 tanks and 60 trucks rolls out of town to the sound of cheering crowds. People gather on street corners to watch the troops leave, shouting "Yeltsin! Yeltsin!" Taxi drivers signal their approval, thumbs-up. Outside the Russian White House, clusters of demonstrators hold transistor radios to their ears to hear the news. Jubilant young men pour beer down each other's throats while crowds of Yeltsin supporters link arms and walk six-abreast through streets that are still blocked by the protesters' impromptu barricades.

"We are not heroes, but we are patriots," a student says. "The first day, we had no faith that we could win. The

Crowds cheer as Soviet tanks pull out of Moscow on the afternoon of August 21.

second day, we began to believe in ourselves. Now we have to understand that we have to fight for ourselves and for our own freedom, that we can't expect Gorbachev or anyone else to do it for us." A young man adds, "We will never again bend our spines to authority the way our fathers did."

The retreating tanks and trucks are filled with grinning eighteen- and nineteen-year-old soldiers. "It's over! We've got our orders," a young tank commander cheers. When they pass three old women selling flowers, the soldiers find themselves pelted with roses. One sergeant grabs one and sticks it in the end of his machine gun as other soldiers wave their combat hats at the crowd, happy that the worst did not happen. They were not ordered to shoot their own people. Despite traffic restrictions, many Moscow residents get into their cars to follow the tanks out of town. "I want to make sure the tanks are really leaving. I'll follow them into their barracks if I have to," one driver says.

Just as the coup itself has been bungled, there are some comically inept incidents during the convoy's retreat. Several tanks get stuck in ditches on the side of the road and have to be dragged out. One troop truck stalls, and three others get flat tires.

Coup Leaders Arrested

On Wednesday afternoon, two airplanes leave Moscow for the Crimea. One carries a band of Yeltsin and Gorbachev supporters. In the other plane are four members of the Emergency Committee: Defense Minister Dmitri Yazov, Deputy Security Council Chairman Oleg Baklanov, the head of the industrialists' union, Nikolai Tizyakov, and KGB chief Vladimir Kryuchkov. The Yeltsin team does not yet know that the coup has failed. Their mission: to ascertain the safety of captive Soviet leader Mikhail Gorbachev and to brief him on the status of the growing resistance movement. While in the air, Yeltsin aides begin to worry that Gorbachev may have been killed and that they, too,

Opposite:
Boris Yeltsin waves the Russian tricolor flag in victory from the balcony of the Russian Federation building. More than 100,000 supporters gathered in front of the building to celebrate the end of the coup.

Mikhail Gorbachev steps off the plane that returned him to Moscow just after midnight on Thursday, August 22. Behind him are his granddaughter Anastasia and wife Raisa.

may be arrested or shot upon landing. Forty armed guards loyal to Yeltsin spend their flight preparing their weapons for a shoot-out. In the end, they decide not to provoke a bloodbath. They leave their weapons on the plane.

The finale looks more like a scene from a low-budget Western than a political thriller. Landing before the Committee's plane, Gorbachev's supporters dash into a waiting convoy of Jeeps and Soviet-made Volga limos for the ride to their leader's villa. There, a weary and pale Mikhail Gorbachev gratefully hugs them. When the coup plotters show up sometime later, Gorbachev has them arrested. Yazov, Baklanov, and Tizyakov are forced to remain under guard in the same house where Gorbachev has spent three terrifying days under house arrest. "They will have a lot of time to think. They won't be going anywhere for a while," Gorbachev says, ordering KGB chief Kryuchkov to return immediately to Moscow on the plane with him.

Before leaving the Crimea, Mikhail Gorbachev phones Boris Yeltsin and leaders in several other Soviet republics to inform them that the coup is over. He also phones President Bush, who expresses relief that the attempt to overthrow Gorbachev has failed. Mr. Bush says that the United States will continue to provide whatever support Mikhail Gorbachev and Boris Yeltsin want. Speaking of Yeltsin's bravery, Bush notes, "He will have a well-earned stature around the world that he might not have had." Mikhail Gorbachev, who owes his freedom and quite possibly his life to Boris Yeltsin, will have to come to terms with the Russian president in the days that follow.

Gorbachev Returns to the Capital

Shortly after midnight on Thursday, August 22, a triumphant and relieved Mikhail Gorbachev arrives back in Moscow. When a camera crew approaches him at the airport, an aide steps in, "Mikhail Sergeyevich is tired." The Soviet president shakes his head, no. "I want to breathe the free air of Moscow," he smiles.

Not long after his arrival back in the capital, Tass issues an announcement: "BULLETIN—GORBACHEV IN FULL CONTROL OF THE COUNTRY."

In a statement read on Soviet television, Gorbachev declares that he is in control of the Soviet Union again and that he is also taking personal control of the armed forces. He does not mention Boris Yeltsin by name but, in his statement, Gorbachev praises the "decisive actions of the democratic forces of the country" for saving the country. In closing, Mikhail Gorbachev promises that he will resume his normal duties in a few days.

Chapter 2

The Fall of Communism

U ntil the coup, the government of the Soviet Union and the Communist party had been one unit. Communism controlled all aspects of everyday Soviet life. Private property practically did not exist—the government owned all the country's land, homes, and factories. The economy was centrally planned and run by state committees. Factory production of items like cars and agricultural production of food were regulated by quotas set by the Communists. The process of supplying food and other consumer items to the public was also under Communist control. In the 1960s and 1970s, under Leonid Brezhnev, corruption and bribery among Communist party bureaucrats made it harder for everyday people to get food and other necessities. The situation worsened under Soviet leaders Yuri Andropov and Konstantin Chernenko, who followed Brezhnev.

Mikhail Gorbachev saw his country deteriorating. After he came to power in 1985, he attempted to change it by reforming the economy and opening up the political climate. But he ran into fierce opposition from Communist party hardliners who did not want to lose their power and privilege. In addition, Gorbachev's economic reforms were not enough to transform the quickly crumbling economy. Shortages of goods and inflation had greatly worsened by

Ironically, the coup leaders quickened the move toward democracy for the Soviet Union

Opposite:
A monument to communist leader Vladimir Lenin is loaded onto a truck after being disassembled in Lithuania.

Corruption and bribery in the Kremlin worsened under Leonid Brezhnev, who headed the Soviet government from 1964 to 1982.

1991. Gorbachev's policy of *glasnost* appeared to have backfired on him, too. Before the coup, liberals like Boris Yeltsin attacked him in public for not being forceful enough in bringing about reforms. Not only did the liberals challenge his authority—they questioned the validity of communism itself.

Four days after the first tanks rolled into Moscow, the coup was, for the most part, completely over. And even though Soviet leader Mikhail Gorbachev had resumed his post, it was as if he presided over an entirely different country. These four days had changed the Soviet Union forever.

Joseph Stalin

During the years 1929 to 1953, Joseph Stalin was the undisputed ruler of the USSR. His reign did much to transform communism in the Soviet Union from a political movement to an authoritarian bureaucracy. The country saw many advances under Stalin, but the dictator also institutionalized terror in the country. He was responsible for ordering the murder of ten to twenty million people.

Born in Soviet Georgia in 1879, Joseph Stalin—whose original name was Iosif Vissarionovich Dzhugashvili—was the only child in his family to survive infancy. A bright and determined child, Stalin grew up headstrong, hotheaded, and independent.

At age twenty-two, Stalin became involved in politics. He plunged into revolutionary work for the Social Democratic party of Georgia. Stalin advanced quickly through the ranks of the revolutionary movement and, by 1917, was poised to help Lenin and the Bolsheviks overthrow the Russian czars. After the success of the revolution, Stalin was positioned in the new regime as a promising leader.

After the death of Lenin in 1924, Stalin fought to assume a leadership position in the Soviet Union. With shrewd use of politics and persuasion, Stalin managed to achieve his goal by 1929. The first part of his reign was characterized by strict rule, but one that brought better methods of industrial management, reestablishment of traditional procedures in the armed forces, more moderate guidelines for the arts and sciences, and a new focus on the family as the basic social unit. As the years went on, however, Stalin grew more strict—even paranoid—and his actions grew harsh. In 1935, he began a series of "purges" that were designed to rid the country of all opposition. Stalin ordered the arrest and murder, not only of known political subversives, but also of personal friends and political comrades. Soon, Stalin was declaring his own relatives (including his wife) enemies of the state.

Stalin's "reign of terror" continued for many years. Throughout the Soviet Union, citizens were arrested without clear reason; many were tortured for confessions or other information. Most were eventually killed. This tragic era in Soviet history created a longlasting fear and suspicion of government on the part of the Soviet people, one that lasts even to this day. It institutionalized almost a slave-master relationship between the masses and their iron-handed leader. This oppression and intimidation came to be recognized as a hallmark of communism for years to come. It would not be until the mid-1980s that the bold ideas and determination of Mikhail Gorbachev began to pave the way for a "new openness" in Soviet society. By August of 1991, that new openness led to another "Russian revolution"; one that spelled the end of communism in the Soviet Union.

Joseph Stalin

Thursday, August 22, 1991

Taking up the reins of government once again, Mikhail Gorbachev's first official act upon returning to Moscow was to fire Deputy Defense Minister General Vladimir Govorov, who was transferred to "unspecified other work," according to the official news agency, Tass. Gorbachev replaced him with Colonel General Boris Pyankov. Govorov was not one of the eight coup leaders, and at first it was unclear why Gorbachev replaced him with Pyankov, an obscure military commander from Siberia. What was clear was that Gorbachev moved swiftly to replace men he considered disloyal with those he could trust. General Mikhail Moiseyev, chief of the Soviet general staff, became the acting defense minister, replacing coup leader Dmitri Yazov, who was in jail. (U.S. officials were not pleased with Moiseyev's appointment because he had been hostile to Gorbachev's proposals to reduce the Soviet military and place it under constitutional control. "I wouldn't want that guy behind me in a dark hall," one U.S. government official commented upon hearing of Moiseyev's new job.)

Gorbachev's other top picks were less controversial to American officials. KGB chief Vladimir Kryuchkov was replaced by Leonid Shebarshin, a career KGB officer responsible for overseas espionage operations. Lt. General Vasily Trushin was named acting interior minister, replacing Boris Pugo, who shot his wife and committed suicide upon being arrested for his role in the coup. (The KGB chief runs the internal security police and both the internal and international espionage operations. The Soviet interior minister is in charge of the general police force.) Mikhail Gorbachev came to power with the help of supporters in the KGB—his mentor, Yuri Andropov, was KGB chief before becoming head of state. Many people thought Gorbachev would use the fallout from the coup as a chance to shake up the KGB power structure. But no matter how many "liberals" Gorbachev appointed, the fact remained

Boris Yeltsin

Defeating the men who sought to seize control of the Soviet Union by force marked the climax of sixty-year-old Boris Yeltsin's extraordinary political career. There have been many times when it looked as if Yeltsin's political future was doomed, but persevering through adversity brought him to a rare position as an internationally recognized leader who shared power with Soviet President Mikhail Gorbachev. (Standing over six feet tall, with a full head of white hair, Boris Yeltsin towered over Mikhail Gorbachev, making it look as if he was the leader of the team.)

Born on February 1, 1931, in Sverdlov, a town in the Ural Mountains, Boris Yeltsin was a daredevil who, at the age of eleven, stole some hand grenades. They exploded, taking off a thumb and part of one finger. After attending engineering school, he held various jobs as a construction engineer from 1955 through 1968, joining the Communist party at the relatively late age of thirty.

In 1976, Boris Yeltsin was appointed first secretary of the Sverdlov District Central Committee. There, he acquired his reputation as a charismatic reformer, unafraid to speak out against Communist policies. This exposed him to the anger of party colleagues. But the people in his district loved Boris Yeltsin for his directness.

Mikhail Gorbachev brought Yeltsin to Moscow in 1985, appointing him secretary of the Central Committee for Construction. Yeltsin immediately gave up his party limousine and took the bus to work. (Unlike Mikhail Gorbachev, who enjoyed the privileges of a high-level

Boris Yeltsin, campaigning for the Russian presidency in June 1991.

Communist party official, Boris Yeltsin prefers to live simply.) Not only was his lifestyle shocking to other party bureaucrats (*apparatchiks*), Yeltsin further outraged his comrades in the Communist party when he made a speech attacking "bureaucracy, social injustice and abuses."

In 1987, Yeltsin resigned from his posts in the Moscow and national Communist party chapters after complaining that the economic reforms of *perestroika* were moving too slowly. He also attacked *apparatchiks* for corruption and inefficiency. Mikhail Gorbachev, who owed his career to supporters in the Communist party, attacked Boris Yeltsin soon after. In 1989, when Yeltsin ran as a delegate to the new Congress of People's Deputies,

Mikhail Gorbachev ran a counter-campaign for anti-Yeltsin votes. But the popular and indomitable Russian won by a landslide.

Fed up with the Communist party, Boris Yeltsin resigned his party membership in July 1990. In June 1991, he was elected president of the Russian Federation by an overwhelming majority. This was the first popular election ever to take place in Russia. Yeltsin was also the first leader in Soviet history to have built his career on the people's support rather than moving up through the ranks of the Communist party. His natural magnetism and warmth, combined with tremendous personal courage, have earned Boris Yeltsin the respect and admiration of people around the world.

that as long as the Soviet secret police agency was not dismantled, it would have tremendous power, including its own army division.)

Having taken care of immediate political business, Mikhail Gorbachev needed now to face his people, and the world. "We have experienced one of the most difficult trials in the entire history of the reforms of our society," he said in his first televised speech since the coup began. Referring to his own ordeal, Gorbachev described his "seventy-two hours of total isolation. Everything was done, I think, to weaken me psychologically. It was hard. I learned some hard lessons. It's hard to say it now, but that's how it was." Confessing his fear that "they might have killed me and my whole family," Gorbachev called his captors "primitive and crude and crafty." He also expressed great disappointment in the men who tried to overthrow him, especially Vice President Gennady Yanayev.

Citing the courageous role of the republics, especially Russia, in resisting the coup, Mikhail Gorbachev publicly praised Boris Yeltsin for the first time. This brought approval from the crowd. His speech was interrupted a number of times as the audience applauded the Russian president. Gorbachev conceded that it was time to heal the rift between them. "We understand now what it means to be united and what it means to be disunited when you are a democracy. And we had in the past practically called one another enemies. Now we can begin to think how we are going to pick up the pieces," Gorbachev observed. Calling on the Soviet people to stand behind him, Gorbachev promised to press on with his reforms. "We must not lose time. We have to move forward and solve our problems. That's the main thing," he concluded.

Yeltsin Cheered at Rally

Later in the day on Thursday, tens of thousands of jubilant people gathered outside the Russian Parliament building to celebrate their freedom. Waving the traditional tricolor flag

On Thursday, August 22, tens of thousands of joyous citizens massed in front of the Russian Parliament to hear Boris Yeltsin praise the efforts of protesters and revel in the defeat of the coup leaders.

of Russia that had been banned since 1917, the people roared approval when a triumphant Boris Yeltsin appeared on the balcony. The hero of the resistance praised them for successfully defeating the junta. "The attempt to change the direction of the development of our country, to cast it into the abyss of violence and lawlessness, has failed," said Yeltsin. From the outset of the shocking coup of Monday, 19, "the country was drowned in a sea of lies." For the next three days and nights, "many thousands of Muscovites demonstrated steadfastness, citizenship, and heroism . . . . Your weapon was the enormous will to defend the ideals of freedom, democracy and human worth."

Noting the need to learn "serious lessons from the past," Yeltsin pointed out "how fragile freedom is in our society, and how vulnerable are democracy and *glasnost*." In fact, he noted, "this is a lesson for us all, including the country's president, Gorbachev. At the same time, it has again been shown how great are the powers of the people."

To Yeltsin, the price of this freedom was "too high . . . the irreplaceable loss of human life, of people killed during the putsch (coup), huge losses in the economy. Still, the

The Power of the KGB

Soviet citizens stand triumphantly around the fallen statue of KGB founder Felix Dzerzhinsky, toppled after the coup failed.

Since its creation more than seventy-four years ago, the KGB has been a powerful force in Soviet society. For much of this time, the KGB has been all-powerful. It has maintained the oppression that characterized most Communist governments.

Originally called the Extraordinary Commission for Combatting Counter-Revolution and Sabotage (or "Cheka"), the secret police agency was founded on December 20, 1917. The agency was the brainchild of Vladimir Lenin, the founder of Soviet communism and leader of the Bolshevik movement that overthrew the Russian czars during the revolution in 1917. That year, Lenin appointed Felix Dzerzhinsky the first head of the organization. "Iron Felix" was known for his fanatical loyalty to Lenin as well as his brutality toward citizens he suspected were subversives. Under his leadership, the Cheka executed millions of people without a trial, and tortured countless others.

The harsh methods of the Cheka were the legacy of later years as well. During the years that Joseph Stalin ruled the USSR (1929-1953) the party-controlled NKVD (forerunner of the KGB) was used to strike fear into the hearts of all citizens. Arrests in the middle of the night, torture of suspected traitors, and murder were all part of the agency's duties during this era. An estimated 20 million people were killed by the agency under Lenin and Stalin combined. Under Stalin's guidance in particular, the NKVD became a massive tool of intimidation and fear.

Under the leadership of Nikita Khrushchev beginning in 1956, the agency, now called the KGB, became somewhat less fearsome. Although its presence was still far-reaching, its duties became more sophisticated. The agency increased international spying operations, creating massive files on everyone from fruit vendors to high government officials. These operations also involved frequent and unexplained interrogations of Soviet citizens, intended, as always, to intimidate people who might have harbored notions of dissent. But the agency, in general, was moving away from senseless brutality and more toward a complex and far-reaching intelligence network.

After Mikhail Gorbachev took power, the role of the KGB began to get blurry. How would an agency with such a history fit into the Soviet Union's new *glasnost* and *perestroika?* Gorbachev knew the KGB would have to change but he was reluctant to tamper with it. After the coup attempt, Gorbachev realized that major changes were required throughout his government, including the KGB. Ex-KGB chief Vladimir Kryuchkov (who was credited as being the mastermind behind the coup) was eventually replaced by Vadim Bakatin, a pro-reform thinker with a peace-loving demeanor. Bakatin's primary task was to change the KGB's image and to restructure the organization so it could function in a society headed for democracy. He began by promising to reduce the agency's spying operations and to cut back on its military arsenal, which included 220,000 uniformed troops (more than the U.S. Marines) and more tanks than the British Army. Bakatin has also changed the agency's name. It is now officially known as the Inter-republican Council for Security, or MSB.

main thing is that the coup failed." Looking to the future, he hoped that "the forces that organized the coup are historically doomed, and first and foremost because the people have already made their choice and do not intend to reject it. The people have already freed themselves from the fear of former years."

Eduard Shevardnadze, the former foreign minister who resigned in December of 1990 warning that the country was facing a dictatorship, addressed the crowd next. He, too, was cheered when he said that those who had given their lives fighting the coup should be treated as heroes and buried inside the Kremlin wall. "If there is no space, then there are people that we can dig out," Shevardnadze bellowed, referring to old Communist heroes. The crowd went wild with approval.

Anti-KGB Demonstrations

Not all the rallies were cheerful on August 22; several hundred people gathered outside the headquarters of the Communist party to vent their anger. Inside, as the Communist party Central Committee held its regular Thursday meeting, the mood was conciliatory. The central committee called for a full investigation into the attempted coup and threatened to revoke membership in the Communist party for those found guilty of trying to overthrow Mikhail Gorbachev. Their decree was especially ironic in light of the fact that several leading Communist party members— the coup plotters themselves—were already in jail.

Along with the Communist party, the official news agency, Tass, and the KGB attempted to conceal their tracks, too, by issuing statements praising the return of Gorbachev. It was a desperate attempt on the part of the Communist establishment to hold onto power.

The new order had clearly arrived. After nightfall, as fireworks burst over Red Square, demonstrators showed that they were not yet finished. Shortly before 11:30 P.M., they commandeered two Moscow city cranes and pulled down a statue outside the headquarters of the dreaded KGB. The statue was a likeness of Felix Dzerzhinsky, founder of the secret police agency responsible for torturing and killing Soviet citizens suspected of being enemies of the state.

The tearing down of the statue of "Iron Felix" symbolized the complete overturn of the old totalitarian system of Soviet government. It was a fitting and powerful end to a day of triumph, celebration, and defiance. Now, more than ever, it seemed as if anything was possible.

Friday, August 23, 1991

Exhilarated by the previous night's events, young demonstrators armed with hammers and chisels returned to KGB headquarters early in the morning of August 23. Having toppled the giant statue of "Iron Felix," they began frantically chiseling away at the statue's base. In a scene reminiscent of the dismantling of the Berlin Wall in Germany, pieces of the KGB founder's statue instantly became prized souvenirs. On the remaining piece of the statue, young people scrawled "Fascists" and "Executioners." One young man, holding a bullhorn, led the crowd in a call to "arrest the big stars of the Mafia," meaning privileged, corrupt government officials.

The urge to destroy more icons of Communist rule spread through the nation. Soon, protesters were tying a noose around the monument of Yakov Sverdlov, the man who, with Vladimir Lenin, assassinated the czar of Russia and his family after the Bolshevik revolution in 1917. In the Estonian capital, Talinn, officials ordered the main statue of Lenin razed.

"Musical Ministers"

With so many new positions to fill, Mikhail Gorbachev seemed to have trouble making up his mind. Ministers appointed one day were being fired and replaced the next. Although he offered no reasons for the newest changes,

Gorbachev had been in closed sessions with Boris Yeltsin, and the new appointments appeared to be a sign of Gorbachev's giving in to Yeltsin's recommendations. These changes signaled an important shift in—and sharing of—the Soviet power base.

Keeping track of the new government appointments was like following a game of musical chairs. It was so confusing that many people wondered who was in charge. General Mikhail Moiseyev, who replaced defense minister Dmitri Yazov, was soon replaced by Air Force Colonel-General Yevgeny Shaposhnikov. Less than twenty-four hours after his appointment, the new head of the KGB, Leonid Shebarshin, was replaced by Vadim Bakatin, Gorbachev's former interior minister. Other victims of "musical ministers" were Foreign Minister Aleksandr Bessmertnykh and Speaker of the Soviet Parliament Anatoly Lukyanov, whose ideology reportedly inspired the coup plotters. The new appointments meant that for the first time, the Soviet Union's vast military and security forces were under the control of people who were considered liberal reformers, rather than hardline Communists. These changes were also expected to have far-reaching implications for Soviet society and for future relations with the rest of the world.

For symbolic value, it was Russian President Boris Yeltsin rather than Soviet President Mikhail Gorbachev who first announced the new ministers. Yeltsin read the list of appointments when he addressed a crowd of demonstrators outside KGB headquarters.

Yeltsin Upstages Gorbachev

Later in the morning, when Gorbachev and Yeltsin appeared together before the Soviet Parliament, it was clear that the balance of power had shifted in Boris Yeltsin's favor. When Gorbachev's limousine pulled up in front of the Russian Parliament building, thousands of protesters shouted "Resign! Resign!" Many held signs calling for his resignation and the end of what they angrily referred to as

"Partocracy," or Communist party rule. Gorbachev's opening remarks, broadcast on television to the crowd assembled outside the Parliament building, were not well received. "Shame! Shame!" the crowd booed.

Inside the packed Parliament chambers, Gorbachev did not seem to be faring much better with the Russian deputies, who heckled him from the audience even after he expressed gratitude to them for resisting the coup. For the second time in two days, Gorbachev gave personal thanks to Boris Yeltsin. What came next was an astonishing realignment of leadership. Gorbachev announced that he and Boris Yeltsin had agreed to a power-sharing arrangement: "If one of us finds himself unable to carry out his duties, then the other will immediately take over his powers."

Agreeing with Gorbachev in principle, Boris Yeltsin went even further when he interrupted the Soviet leader to declare, "And now for a bit of relaxation. Let me sign a decree suspending the activity of the Russian Communist party." Gorbachev, stunned, started to stammer, "Boris Nikolayevich, Boris Nikolayevich." Yeltsin interrupted him again with a smirk. "It's been signed," he announced with a flourish as the deputies burst into cheers and applause. Clearly flustered, Gorbachev attempted to explain his belief that the Communist party could be salvaged and reformed. But he had already "lost face" to Boris Yeltsin, who relished gaining emotional and political control.

Gorbachev Fires the Soviet Government

Yeltsin continued to command the session when, once again, he stopped Gorbachev from explaining what had occurred during the coup. In a sarcastic tone, Yeltsin interjected, "Sometimes Mikhail Sergeyevich forgets things."

In order to impress upon Gorbachev the full extent to which his ministers had betrayed him in the past week, Yeltsin handed over the minutes of a closed session of the Council of Ministers. During that meeting, which took

Boris Yeltsin shows Mikhail Gorbachev the minutes from the meeting where the Soviet president's Council of Ministers voted to overthrow Gorbachev.

place on Monday, August 19, nearly all of his ministers voted to overthrow Mikhail Gorbachev.

Faced with the document, the Soviet president was embarrassed. "I haven't read this yet," he stammered.

"Go ahead, read it now," Yeltsin ordered Gorbachev in front of the entire Parliament.

Upon reading the minutes, Mikhail Gorbachev was forced to confront the truth. The people whom he trusted, those who had claimed to support *glasnost* and *perestroika*, had stabbed him in the back. With a creeping tone of despair and hopelessness in his voice, Gorbachev announced, "The whole government has got to resign. I must say this has been a great drama for me, a severe trial."

It was a moment of personal triumph for Boris Yeltsin. In 1987, when Yeltsin was in the hospital, he had been summoned by Gorbachev to face an angry meeting of the Moscow Communist party Central Committee. At issue was Yeltsin's public criticism of the Communist party and its Politburo. (The Politburo is the Communist "congress," although members are not elected. It does, however, debate and decide the Soviet Union's goals and policies.) During that meeting, speaker after speaker had denounced Yeltsin's "political immaturity." In 1990, Gorbachev had called on the Russian Parliament to vote against Yeltsin because of his "anti-Communist remarks." In a peculiar twist of political fate, it looked as if the two liberal reformers would be spending their careers attacking each other instead of collaborating to achieve a joint goal. But in the spring of 1990, they seemed to be moving toward a reconciliation when they opened negotiations for the new union treaty that would have given much greater powers to the country's fifteen republics.

Gorbachev had clearly lost some of his stature after his parliamentary encounter with Boris Yeltsin. Upon leaving the building, he was jeered and pushed by angry and emotional members of the crowd.

For his part, Yeltsin had emerged empowered. On the afternoon of the Parliament meeting, he fired the heads of

Communist Party Highlights

1848 Germans Karl Marx and Friedrich Engels coin the term "communism" in *The Communist Manifesto*, a blueprint for future revolutionaries. (Marx and Engels first conceived of communism as a means by which all members of a society could share all things equally.)

1867 Marx publishes *Das Kapital*, a manifesto for communism. Under Marx's system, every member of a communist society would contribute according to his or her abilities, and would be compensated according to his or her needs by the Communist state.

1898 First congress of the Russian Social-Democratic Labor party (RSDLP) in Minsk.

1903 Second congress of the Russian Social-Democratic Labor party. Vladimir Ilyich Lenin forms a breakaway faction, the Bolsheviks. The Menshevik revolutionary faction loses its power base.

1917 In February, the Russian Revolution deposes Czar Nicholas II, bringing the rule of monarchy to an end. In November, the Bolsheviks successfully mount a coup and seize control of the new government. Vladimir Lenin becomes the first Soviet head of state.

1918 The Russian Social-Democratic Labor party changes its name to the Russian Communist party. The Communists ban all other political parties and wage war against all anti-Bolshevik forces.

1924 Vladimir I. Lenin dies. In his last will and testament, Lenin opposes Joseph Stalin as his successor. But Stalin soon emerges as the new Communist party leader and head of the Soviet Union.

1934 Leningrad Communist party leader Sergei Kirov is assassinated, causing Joseph Stalin to purge "disloyal" Communist party members. Through the 1930s, more than ten million Soviet citizens are killed by Stalinists. As part of the purges, Stalin uses force to impose collective (centrally run) farming by seizing privately held land.

1952 The party gets a new name: the Communist party of the Soviet Union.

1953 Joseph Stalin dies. Nikita Khrushchev becomes Communist party leader.

1957 Although Khrushchev denounces Stalin in 1956, he becomes the Soviet premier.

1964 Leonid Brezhnev becomes the chairman of the Supreme Soviet and new head of state.

1982 Leonid Brezhnev dies. Yuri Andropov becomes Communist party leader and head of state.

1984 Yuri Andropov dies. Konstantin Chernenko becomes Communist party leader and head of state.

1985 Konstantin Chernenko dies. Mikhail Gorbachev becomes Communist party leader and head of state. He institutes a policy of reform that includes *glasnost* (openness) and *perestroika* (privatization of the economy).

1988 Mikhail Gorbachev's reforms extend to the political process as he introduces Communist party elections with multiple candidates and a parliament. For the first time since 1918, non-Communist candidates may run for office.

1989 First elections are held for a representative parliament, called the Congress of People's Deputies. The 2,250-seat Congress now elects the Supreme Soviet, a parliament of selected delegates that has greater legislative authority. In the past, parliaments were tools of the Communist party, but the new Congress is vocal in debating and opposing some official Communist-sponsored programs. For the first time, nearly one third of Communist party delegates are defeated by non-party candidates and Congressional debates are broadcast live on television.

1990 Congress of People's Deputies votes to amend the Constitution, removing the article that gives the Communist party a "leading role" in society. Congress elects Mikhail Gorbachev as president of the Soviet Union. The Communist party votes to separate the party activities from government. Boris Yeltsin and several supporters leave the Communist party.

1991 Mikhail Gorbachev calls for a new Communist party Congress. He proposes that free enterprise replace the centrally controlled economy and rejects Marxism-Leninism. This angers Communist hardliners who attempt to overthrow the Soviet president in a coup that fails. After the coup, Mikhail Gorbachev resigns as general secretary of the Communist party and calls for the Communist party Central Committee to dissolve itself.

Soviet television and the official news agency, Tass, after accusing them of spreading "disinformation" about the coup. Yeltsin also banned publication of the official Communist party newspaper *Pravda*. As president of Russia, Boris Yeltsin did not have the official authority to intervene in the running of the national media. But, with the lines of command now blurry, Yeltsin moved into new domains.

Communist Party Shut Down

"Down with the party! Down with the party!" The chant filled the street outside Soviet Communist party Central Committee headquarters in Moscow where two thousand people prepared to break in. They were looking for documents that might connect members of the Communist party with the coup. As if in response to the crowd's command, Russian police officers posted a large notice on the door: "Building Sealed."

Similar scenes were repeated throughout the Soviet Union. In the restless Baltic states, thousands of demonstrators staged candelight vigils in support of independence from the Soviet Union. Latvia joined Lithuania in banning the Communist party. Lithuanian police occupied Communist party headquarters and Lithuanian President Vitautas Landsbergis called for the arrest of Communist party members who supported the coup. In the Ukraine, Communist President Leonid Kravchuk resigned in response to a growing tide of opposition. In Georgia, officials prepared to ban the Communist party and nationalize its property. Moldavian First Secretary Grigory Yeremey informed Gorbachev of his plans to resign from the Politburo, following in the footsteps of Uzbekistan President Islam Karimov.

Throughout the Russian republic, Boris Yeltsin's decrees had a wide-ranging impact. Communist party activity was banned in the KGB, the Soviet military, and the Interior Ministry. Yeltsin also ordered the nationalization of Communist party-owned printing plants.

On Friday, August 23, a large crowd of demonstrators gathered in front of Moscow's Communist party Central Committee headquarters. The angry citizens were going to break into the building before it was sealed off to the public.

By Friday evening, August 23, the mood outside the Communist party headquarters in Moscow was jubilant. Musicians and Cossack folk dancers performed impromptu entertainment with traditional Russian instruments for the crowd of several hundred people who remained gathered outside the building, as night fell.

Saturday, August 24, 1991

One of the first indications that life in the Soviet Union would be truly different could be seen at Moscow news-stands early on the morning of the 24th. Or rather, not seen. For the first time since 1917, *Pravda*, the official newspaper of the Communist party, did not appear. Nor did the five other party newspapers that Boris Yeltsin ordered to be closed down.

Saturday was declared an official day of mourning. Traffic in downtown Moscow was hopelessly snarled as hundreds of thousands of people marched through the streets to honor the three young demonstrators who had been killed on Tuesday night. As they gathered in the cemetery where the founder of Soviet communism, Vladimir Lenin, had been previously buried, the demonstrators mourned the deaths of the three young men. But they also celebrated the death of the political system that Lenin founded.

On August 24, citizens mourned the deaths of three young demonstrators who were killed during a skirmish between protesters and the military on the second night of the coup.

It was a diverse crowd. Soviet war veterans who served in Afghanistan, blue-collar workers, and government officials all flocked together. The three coffins were covered by the newly resurrected flag of Russia, flanked by Russian Orthodox priests and a rabbi. The open presence of clergymen at a public gathering was another sign that communism was disappearing. The official policy of the Communist party is atheistic. Freedom of religion was denied until Mikhail Gorbachev relaxed restrictions on worship as part of *glasnost.*

People in the crowd were exhilarated by their newfound freedom and appeared to enjoy themselves. For years, the Soviet people censored themselves out of fear. Now, a humorous new slogan was making the rounds: "If it is forbidden, then we must do it." "We are not going back," yelled Dmitri Lyuty, a veteran who fought in Afghanistan. Lyuty was among those who formed the human barricades around the Russian Parliament building earlier that week.

As part of the solemn ceremony, Mikhail Gorbachev eulogized the three young men who had given their lives for the resistance. "I feel indebted to the memory of these young people who gave their lives in blocking the way to those who wanted to smash democracy and return the country to the gloomy times. I bow low to them for all that they did," he said, adding that those who plotted to overthrow him, "will get what they deserve. There will be no forgiveness."

Leonid Kravchuk, president of the Ukraine, was forced to resign his office due to the serious anti-Communist sentiment in his country.

Ukraine Declares Independence

In Kiev on Saturday, ten thousand people waving the blue and yellow flags of the nationalist movement converged on the Ukrainian Parliament. It was there and then that the Ukrainian government declared its independence from the Soviet Union and claimed control over 1.5 million Soviet troops stationed on Ukrainian soil. With twenty-one percent of the Soviet population, the Ukraine is the second most important Soviet republic after Russia. It provides the nation with twenty-five precent of its food and coal and accounts for twenty-one percent of its industry.

Saturday's decision was the most serious blow to the proposed union treaty. It threatened the complete break-up of the Soviet Union. The 50 million people who live in the Ukraine were scheduled to vote on the declaration of independence by December 1991. With a strong nationalist movement, the Ukraine historically has fought against Soviet domination. Many Ukrainian freedom fighters, called dissidents, have served time in KGB prisons and Siberian labor camps. A December vote to approve separate national status would merely confirm a longstanding desire to be free of the Soviet Union.

Baltic Republics Declare Independence

On the coast of the Baltic Sea, in the northeastern corner of the Soviet Union, the Baltic Republics—Lithuania, Latvia, and Estonia—celebrated the collapse of the coup. Although the Baltic republics are comparatively small, they have strong ethnic identities. Since being forcibly annexed by Joseph Stalin in 1940, the peoples of the Baltic states have considered themselves "occupied" and have wanted their freedom. Over the years, Baltic dissidents have suffered torture by the KGB and long years of exile in Siberian labor camps because of their beliefs.

Lithuania (population 3.7 million) declared independence from the Soviet Union on March 11, 1990, but Mikhail Gorbachev sent in troops and soon squashed the movement. Lithuania later joined Estonia (population 1.6 million) on Tuesday, August 20, 1991, when both republics proclaimed independence. Latvia (population 2.7 million) declared independence on Wednesday, August 21, 1991. Within a month, the new Baltic nations received full recognition by more than a dozen other nations, including the United States and the Russian Federation.

Just how the Soviet Union would respond to these new nations remained unclear. In the old system, the

THE FIFTEEN REPUBLICS OF THE SOVIET UNION

Area of large map

D.I. = Declared Independence

DENMARK

SWEDEN

GERMANY

BALTIC SEA

ESTONIA
Pop. 1.6 mil.
D.I. 8/20/91

FINLAND

POLAND

LITHUANIA
Pop. 3.7 mil.
D.I. 3/11/90

LATVIA
Pop. 2.7 mil.
D.I. 8/21/91

BYELORUSSIA
Pop. 10.2 mil.
D.I. 8/25/91

MOLDAVIA
Pop. 4.3 mil.
D.I. 8/27/91

ROMANIA

Moscow

UKRAINE
Pop. 51.7 mil.
D.I. 8/24/91

RUSSIA
(Detail)

BLACK SEA

GEORGIA
Pop. 5.4 mil.
D.I. 4/9/91

TURKEY

KAZAKHSTAN
Pop. 16.5 mil.
Not independent
as of 12/91

ARMENIA
Pop. 3.3 mil.
Not independent
as of 12/91

CASPIAN SEA

ARAL
SEA

UZBEKISTAN
Pop. 19.9 mil.
D.I. 8/31/91

LAKE
BALKHASH

IRAQ

AZERBAIJAN
Pop. 7 mil.
D.I. 8/30/91

KIRGHIZIA
Pop. 2.7 mil.
D.I. 8/21/91

TURKMENISTAN
Pop. 3.6 mil.
Not independent
as of 12/91

IRAN

TADZHIKISTAN
Pop. 5.1 mil.
Not independent
as of 12/91

CHINA

0   500 mi.

0   800 km.

AFGHANISTAN

Baltics were important to the Soviet economy because of
their shipbuilding, electrical, and construction industries.
As independent nations, they no longer had any authorized
ties to the Soviet government. More republics seemed
likely to declare their independence and separate from the
central system. Thus the Soviet Union would no longer

exist as it did before. There was even a possibility that civil war could erupt in the breakaway republics. It was unclear what role the new Soviet government would play as the old system gave way.

Gorbachev Resigns from Communist Party

The highlight of Saturday's events occurred late in the day when Mikhail Gorbachev resigned as general secretary of the Communist party. He also ordered the Soviet government to seize all Communist party property. (Until that time, the Communist party and the Soviet government had been virtually the same entity).

"The Communist party Central Committee should take the difficult but honest decision to dissolve itself," Mikhail Gorbachev stated, calling on "democratically minded Communists" to create "a new party of renewal."

It was clear that the Soviet president had been irrevocably affected by the thorough betrayal of his political comrades. "Members of the party leadership were among the conspirators. A number of party committees and media supported the actions of state criminals." Therefore, he said, "I do not consider it possible to continue to carry out the functions of the general secretary of the Communist party Central Committee, and I surrender those powers."

Within a few short days, the Soviet system had undergone an upheaval that many people called "the second Russian revolution." With this revolution, the communist way of life came to an abrupt end after more than sixty years. In fact, there are very few people alive in the Soviet Union who remember any other way of living.

In the ashes of the old system, an entirely new way of life was born. This means that in decades to come, the Soviet nation will have to create a new political, economic, and social structure. The big challenge will be finding a way to ensure stability while the economic and social reforms take effect.

The third Russian revolution is about to begin.

Mikhail Gorbachev

Considered one of the most important political figures of the twentieth century, Mikhail Gorbachev surprised the world when he became the leader of the Soviet Union in 1985. As general secretary of the Communist party, Gorbachev was a career party official, an *apparatchik* known for his personal charm and ability to compromise with warring power factions. Few people expected this stocky, balding man to end the Cold War, win the Nobel Peace Prize in 1990, and begin a process of drastic social reform at home that would ultimately lead to the complete collapse of Soviet communism.

Mikhail ("Misha") Sergeyevich Gorbachev was born during a time of famine on March 2, 1931, in a village called Privolnoe in the south of Russia. Most of his family, who were farmers, survived the Stalinist purges of the 1930s. But Gorbachev's grandfather, Andrei Gorbachev, was sent to a Siberian work camp in the vast system called the *gulag*. This apparently had a strong impact on Mikhail, who joined the Communist party as a young man. For years, Gorbachev was ashamed of his grandfather's arrest, fearing that it would hurt his political career. But when he felt the time was right, he restored his grandfather's honor, in part by making sweeping changes in the repressive policies left over from Stalin's era.

After graduating from Moscow State University, where he met and married Raisa Maksimovna, Mikhail Gorbachev returned to the south of Russia, where he became a party leader in his home district of

Mikhail Gorbachev

Stavropol. There, during Leonid Brezhnev's regime (nicknamed "the era of stagnation"), Gorbachev earned a reputation for honesty. Although corruption was rampant, Gorbachev refused payoffs.

As first secretary of the Stavropol region, it was his task to accompany party leaders from Moscow when they visited the thermal spas in his district. This was how he met KGB chief Yuri Andropov. Andropov was impressed with Gorbachev's intellect and education. The two men often went for long walks in the woods where they could speak freely without being overheard or "bugged." Although Gorbachev had already begun to befriend writers who were considered dissidents, or enemies of the state, he was able to balance his friendship with the KGB director who was responsible for their imprisonment. This ability to accept contradictions, even when they appeared to go against his principles, enabled Mikhail Gorbachev to rise through the ranks of the Communist party relatively quickly. As a protege of Yuri Andropov, Mikhail Gorbachev also had the support of Foreign Minister

Andrei Gromyko, who nominated Gorbachev as general secretary of the Communist party in 1985.

When he first took office as general secretary, Mikhail Gorbachev believed that he could improve the faltering Soviet economy by boosting private enterprise. He also believed that he could restructure the Communist party so that it would be more responsive to the needs of the people. He began a two-pronged program of reform called *perestroika* (economic reform) and *glasnost* (openness). But the Soviet economy was in such a state of crisis that *perestroika* often seemed like too little, too late. *Glasnost*, too, was creating repercussions for the Soviet leader. As more people became openly critical of the Communist party, some, like Russian Federation President Boris Yeltsin, openly rebelled. This, in turn, produced a backlash by Communist hardliners who feared losing control. Mikhail Gorbachev found himself the target of criticism by hardliners, who thought he was too liberal, and progressives, like Yeltsin who thought he was too soft. He was also attacked for his lavish lifestyle—Gorbachev had four expensive homes—which was seen as an insult to the millions of Soviet citizens struggling to make ends meet.

In the wake of the coup, the Soviet system collapsed completely. This led to Gorbachev's resignation. But his magnetism, his passion for freedom, his commitment to peace, and his intelligence had ensured that he would win a place in the history of his country and the world.

Chapter 3

The Old Order Breaks Down

In the wake of Mikhail Gorbachev's decision to dissolve the Communist party, the Soviet Union itself began to collapse. One after the other, the fifteen republics that formed the Union of Soviet Socialist Republics seceded— or resolved to secede—from the old order. First the Baltic states—Latvia, Lithuania, and Estonia—declared their independence. Gorbachev and Yeltsin were quick to recognize their independence. Dozens of other world leaders, among them President Bush, acknowledged the new nations, as well.

While this trend meant greater freedom for the people at large, it threatened the very existence of the Soviet Union. Warning that the nation was "on the brink of catastrophe," Gorbachev and leaders of ten republics went before the Congress of People's Deputies to propose a new kind of Soviet Union. What kind, exactly, was still unclear.

First, an emergency interim government would be established, consisting of a state council headed by Gorbachev and the leaders of the fifteen republics. The legislative council would be made up of two chambers of parliament. In the Council of the Republics, each republic would get to seat twenty to fifty-two deputies, or legislators. But each republic can have only one vote. In the Council of Union, the lower house, each republic would

No one is exactly sure what the Soviet Union of the future will be

Opposite:
Lithuania's president, Vitautas Landsbergis, achieved independence for his country in 1991. The other two Baltic Republics of Latvia and Estonia did the same.

have a delegation proportionate to its population. An Inter-Republican Economic Committee would be formed, consisting of an unspecified number of representatives from each republic. The Economic Committee would oversee the day-to-day-running of the Soviet economy and would plan economic reforms. This would mean that both the Supreme Soviet and the Congress of People's Deputies, the first elected congress in Soviet history, would have to be dissolved. Although military and security forces would remain centralized, the republics would have independent nation status. Each new country would apply to the United Nations for its own U.N. seat. Part of the interim government's task would be to work out a permanent structure.

Although they still appeared uneasy together, Mikhail Gorbachev and Boris Yeltsin joined together in urging the Congress of People's Deputies to pass the emergency proposal quickly, before the political disintegration spread throughout Soviet society. That disintegration threatened to destroy the economic links that tied the fifteen republics together. Still critical of Gorbachev, Yeltsin nonetheless praised him for having emerged from his ordeal "a different man," one who could be trusted to lead the country through its next series of crises.

Yevgeny Shaposhnikov became the new Soviet defense minister in 1991.

Vadim Bakatin was appointed by Gorbachev and Yeltsin in 1991 to head up the KGB and to "purge" the agency of old-time Communist hardliners.

Revamping the KGB and the Military

Responsibility for sweeping out the old KGB members who opposed *glasnost* fell to the new head of the secret police agency, Vadim Bakatin. Announcing a purge of those who supported the coup, Bakatin described the "old" KGB as "uncontrolled by anything and anyone." He said that its monopoly on power caused it to turn against Soviet leader Gorbachev and the state. That statement, in itself, was revolutionary. Bakatin went on to say, "The services of secret informers will not be employed by us, and we will not use that term."

The military is undergoing a minor revolution, as well. The new defense minister, Yevgeny Shaposhnikov, has said that the Soviet Army will become more professional. With the abolition of the Communist party, the military will no longer be intertwined with party activities.

The collapse of communism has also brought certain ironies. People who once enjoyed privileged status now find themselves ostracized socially and politically. "I never thought I'd be out on the street, accused of being a member of a criminal organization," one career party official said in an interview.

Chapter 4

New Global Alliances

Fear of communism has been an important element in American foreign policy since the end of World War II, when the Soviet Union became a nuclear power. The Cold War between the United States and the Soviet Union (1950s to 1980s) had been a psychological war of nerves waged under the threat of nuclear extermination. During the 1950s, Americans built bomb shelters and practiced air raid drills in case the Russians attacked. "Better dead than red" became a popular slogan among those who feared a Communist invasion.

The Cold War climate began to thaw in the early 1970s after President Richard Nixon and Leonid Brezhnev signed the first SALT treaty limiting strategic nuclear weapons. The "thaw," called "detente," did not eliminate many people's suspicion that the goal of Soviet communism was world domination. Ronald Reagan called the Soviet Union "the evil empire" when he campaigned. But, as president, he personally admired Soviet leader Mikhail Gorbachev and supported arms control negotiations.

A New Age of U.S.–Soviet Relations

After the coup, with communism destroyed from within, relations between the United States and the Soviet Union

The failure of
the coup marked
the end of the
Cold War

Opposite:
A sea of Soviet citizens, waving victory signs, celebrate the birth of democracy in their country.

entered a new age. Three weeks after the failed coup, U.S. Secretary of State James Baker went to Moscow seeking a new alliance. By the end of September, President Bush outlined a dramatic blueprint to eliminate nuclear warheads and reduce stockpiles of nuclear weapons. Citing developments in the Soviet Union as a positive sign, Bush said, "We can now take steps to make the world a less dangerous place than ever before in a nuclear age."

The U.S. proposals called for the United States to dismantle more than half of its nuclear arsenal, including weapons aboard navy surface ships and ground-based artillery shells. In announcing the cuts, Bush called on the Soviet Union "to go down the road with us." Specifically, President Bush wanted the Soviets to dismantle all ground-based nuclear weapons, nuclear warheads for short-range ballistic missiles, nuclear air defense missiles, plus nuclear artillery shells, and land mines. He also wanted them to remove all nuclear weapons from submarines and ships. The size of the Soviet nuclear arsenal is difficult to estimate. According to *Time* magazine, the Soviets have 27,000 nuclear warheads. *Newsweek* estimates that the Soviets have 11,570 nuclear warheads and 2,357 nuclear missiles in contrast to the United States' estimated 10,602 nuclear warheads and 1,592 nuclear missiles.

Shortly before issuing this dramatic announcement, President Bush conferred with Mikhail Gorbachev and Russian Federation President Boris Yeltsin by phone. Yeltsin said that "substantial and adequate measures" would be an appropriate Soviet response. Gorbachev has campaigned for an end to all nuclear weapons by the year 2000. Promising to study the U.S. proposals and come up with a reciprocal offer, Gorbachev took the credit for introducing "new thinking" into the global political arena, saying, ". . . this initiative . . . wouldn't have become possible if the Soviet Union hadn't adopted the policy of new thinking, if it hadn't said goodbye to the Cold War and hadn't started moving toward a new type of international relations. These are interrelated issues."

PROPOSED U.S. NUCLEAR REDUCTIONS

Nuclear warheads as of June 1991	Number to be eliminated
ARTILLERY SHELLS 1,740	1,740
LAND-BASED SHORT-RANGE MISSILES 1,250	1,250
NAVAL WEAPONS 1,850	Number to be stored or eliminated 1,850
BOMBER WEAPONS 4,000	Number to be stored for use within 24 hrs. 4,000
SINGLE-WARHEAD INTERCONTINENTAL BALLISTIC MISS. 450	Number to be eliminated 450
MULTIPLE-WARHEAD INTERCONTINENTAL BALLISTIC MISS. 2,000	Number to be eliminated ? Development of the mobile MX Peacekeeper and the mobile option for the Midgetman missile will be abandoned.
SUBMARINE-LAUNCH BALLISTIC WARHEADS 5,400	No change

Gorbachev's counteroffer came one week later with even greater planned reductions than the U.S. proposal. The Soviets offered to eliminate nuclear tactical missile warheads, nuclear artillery, and some surface-to-air (SAM) missiles. Naval nuclear weapons would be eliminated entirely. Development of short-range nuclear bombers would be halted. So would nuclear testing, for a period of one year. The Soviets also proposed reducing their strategic weapons to five thousand. This is one thousand less than the quota outlined in the START treaty of July 1991. Gorbachev also promised to withdraw nuclear weapons from the newly independent republics. The chance of political instability there during the early 1990s had caused concern about nuclear war breaking out. Even the acknowledged independence of these republics by 1991 did not erase fears. In all, the proposed arms reductions represented the biggest drop since the arms race first began.

WHERE COMMUNISM REMAINS

Withdrawal from Cuba

With communism dead in the Soviet Union, other nations were also affected. The first casualty of the post-coup era was Cuba. For more than three decades, the Soviet Union had supported Cuban Communist leader Fidel Castro. Several weeks after the coup, Gorbachev announced that the Soviet Union would withdraw thousands of troops from Cuba and would cut economic ties, as well. U.S. Secretary of State James Baker called this a "very substantial" gesture. He was also pleased with the Soviet decision to halt arms shipments to Afghanistan. (The Soviets withdrew their troops from Afghanistan in 1989, and propped up a puppet leader, President Najibullah.) Maintaining a military presence in these countries was expensive. Reducing the military was more than a gesture of peace. It was a practical move toward freeing up money and brain power needed to solve pressing economic problems.

Chapter 5

Looking Toward the Future

F rom Moscow to Washington, from Kazakhstan to Cuba, the shock waves of those six days in August reverberated around the world. The center of global politics shifted away from communism and toward democracy. But at home, the leaders of the new Soviet confederation were faced with some overwhelming problems. Unless they were able to stop the Soviet economy from disintegrating, and if they were unable to forge new alliances among the fifteen republics, they would face the threat of yet another coup, perhaps within a few months, according to some Soviet experts. "The game is not over. If there is not dramatic change, in a short time, some other hardliner group will be plotting," noted Dimitri Simes, a Soviet expert at the Carnegie Foundation. Jerry Hough, director of the East-West Center at Duke University, predicted, "If the chaos continues, you'll have a coup led by younger generals frustrated by what they perceive as civilian politicians impeding progress. And the next time, the populace might be more willing to buy the idea that an iron hand is needed."

Another factor in the political equation was the shaky alliance between Mikhail Gorbachev and Boris Yeltsin. "The key to the Soviet Union's future depends on whether or not the two can work out and maintain a partnership,"

By the end of 1991, the Soviet Union had ceased to exist

Opposite:
Gorbachev and Yeltsin shake hands after a meeting in the Russian Parliament building. The two men came together from very different political backgrounds to share the leadership of the Soviet Union.

observed Soviet expert Arnold Horlick of the Rand Corporation. Despite his position as head of state, Mikhail Gorbachev was not an elected leader. He had yet to test the will of the people by running for office in a free election. Yeltsin, on the other hand, had already won that challenge. It was the basis of his growing power base.

In addition, the Soviet government was in deep financial trouble. It went bankrupt in November. Russia took over the central government's budget tasks, including paying officials and the military.

A New Commonwealth of Independent States

The final blow to the center came in December, when the Ukraine confirmed its independence in its scheduled referendum. Without the Ukraine, there could be no union. A week after the vote, Yeltsin and the leaders of the Ukraine and Byelorussia announced the formation of a new commonwealth—the Commonwealth of Independent States—centered in Minsk, in Byelorussia. Other republics were invited to join. Members would be independent, but they would cooperate in defense and other areas. President Gorbachev resigned on December 25, and the old Soviet system ceased to exist.

It was not clear if the commonwealth would succeed where the old union had failed. But in the years ahead, the real test will come not in the halls of government but in the streets of Moscow, where people spend several hours a

The gradual changeover from communism to democracy will not be easy for most citizens. The economy will be in disarray as a free-market system takes over, meaning probable shortages of food and everyday necessities for many people.

day lined up to buy basic supplies like meat, sugar, matches, and toilet paper. On one Moscow street, chic designers have boutiques. Down the block, people stand in line for hours for food and clothing.

Inflation is running at one thousand percent. A kilogram (two pounds) of tomatoes that cost a few cents in the late 1980s cost more than a day's wages for the average worker in 1990. Food, work, and survival are the basic issues facing millions of people. "Life is bad, both with clothes and food," says Vasily Sazonov, a welder in an automobile factory. Some Muscovites have taken to hoarding toilet paper and trading it on the large black market for food. Throughout the new republics, millions faced starvation in 1991–92 after a poor wheat-growing season.

Even under a hopeful new leadership, the quality of life in most areas is hard for Americans to understand. Housing shortages force several families to squeeze into small apartments, sharing kitchen and bathroom facilities with people crammed into other apartments. Often, there is no electricity or hot water. Commuting to work across Moscow can take more than an hour and a half because the bus service is so unreliable.

Bribing officials is an important part of daily life. In order to get their children into a good elementary school, parents must bribe the authorities. If a mother wants to be sure her baby is fed while she is at work, she must bribe the day-care center workers. Queuing, or standing in line, can consume up to six hours a day. After waiting three hours to buy sausages and another three hours for milk, a seventy-five-year-old Moscow woman offered a jaded commentary on Soviet life to an interviewer: "All our lives we have been queuing and queuing. We hoped in our old age we would live well. Now we can only hope that things will get better."

Millions of people share that hope. The success of the third Russian revolution will depend on whether or not the new government can succeed in turning such dreams into everyday reality without sacrificing freedom.

Chronology

**Monday,
August 19** 6 A.M. News bulletin announces that Vice President Gennady Yanayev has taken over the duties of president of the USSR.

The Emergency Committee bans all meetings of political parties; closes independent newspapers.

Tanks roll into Moscow.

**Tuesday,
August 20** Thousands gather around the Russian Parliament building to show support for Yeltsin.

By the afternoon, several coup leaders are reported to have "fallen ill."

Baltic Republics of Estonia and Lithuania (again) declare independence from the Soviet Union.

**Wednesday,
August 21** The first shots are fired by Soviet troops just after midnight.

Three men are killed in clashes with troops.

10 A.M. Emergency Committee members give up.

Troops and tanks begin pulling out of Moscow.

Latvia declares its independence from Moscow.

Gorbachev has the coup plotters arrested.

**Thursday,
August 22** Gorbachev returns to Moscow.

Gorbachev concedes that he must work together with Yeltsin.

**Friday,
August 23** Gorbachev announces that he and Yeltsin have agreed to a power-sharing arrangement; calls for the entire government to resign.

Yeltsin fires the heads of Soviet television and bans publication of *Pravda*.

Communist party headquarters is shut down and the party is banned.

**Saturday,
August 24** The Ukrainian government declares its independence.

Gorbachev resigns from the Communist party and orders the seizure of all Communist party property.

For Further Reading

Kronenwetter, Michael. *The New Eastern Europe.* New York: Franklin Watts, 1991.

Resnick, Abraham. *The Union of Soviet Socialist Republics.* Chicago: Childrens Press, 1990.

Tyler, T. *Soviet Union.* Austin: Raintree-Steck-Vaughn, 1991.

World Leaders Past and Present (series). *Gorbachev.* Broomall: Chelsea House, 1990.

Yost, Graham. *The KGB.* New York: Facts On File, 1991.

Index

Afghanistan, 20, 45, 57
Andropov, Yuri, 29, 32, 42, 49

Bakatin, Vadim, 36, 39, 53
Baker, James, 56, 57
Baklanov, Oleg, 7, 24, 26
Baltic Republics
    independence of, 43, 46, 51
BBC, 11, 13
"Beijing Spring," 16
Bessmertnykh, Aleksandr, 19, 39
Bolsheviks, 31, 36, 42
    1917 revolution, 11, 38
Brezhnev, Leonid, 29, 30, 42,
    55
Bush, George, 8, 11, 12, 17,
    27, 51
    proposed reduction of
        nuclear weapons, 56
Byelorussia, 60

Castro, Fidel, 57
Chernenko, Konstantin, 29
Cold War, 49, 55, 56
Commonwealth of
    Independent States, 60
Communist rule, 19
    of U.S.S.R., 18, 29, 31, 49
Communist party Central
    Committee, 41, 48
Congress of People's Deputies,
    42, 51, 52
Council of the Republics (see
    Soviet Republics)
Council of Union (see Soviet
    Republics)
Cuba, 57, 59

Das Kapital, 42
Dzerzhinsky, Felix, 36, 38

Emergency Committee (see
    State Committee for the
    State of Emergency)

Engels, Friedrich, 42

Georgia, Soviet, 43
Glasnost, 30, 34, 36, 41, 42,
    45, 53
    definition of, 6
Gorbachev, Andrei (grandfa-
    ther), 49
Gorbachev, Mikhail
    and Boris Yeltsin, 8, 17, 33,
        35, 39–40, 41, 49, 51,
        52, 59
    and coup attempt, 5–16,
        20–24, 26–27
    dissolution of Communist
        party, 42, 48, 51
    early career, 49
    firing of hardline ministers,
        32, 38–39, 40–41, 43
    and future of Soviet Union,
        24, 34, 60
    and independence move-
        ment, 15, 46
    marriage to Raisa
        Maksimovna, 49
    nuclear reductions, 57
    opposition by hardliners, 18,
        21, 24, 37, 41, 53
    reform policies, 30, 31, 36,
        42, 45, 49
    relationship with U.S., 51,
        55, 56
    resignation from Commu-
        nist party, 42, 48
    rise to power, 29, 42, 49
    supporters of, 24, 26
    and Yuri Andropov, 49
Gorbachev, Raisa (wife), 13,
    26, 49
Govorov, Vladimir, 32
Gromyko, Andrei, 49
Gulag, 49

Havel, Vaclav, 11

Horlick, Arnold, 60
Hough, Jerry, 59

Inter-republican Council for
    Security (see KGB)
Inter-Republican Economic
    Committee (see Soviet
    Republics)

Karimov, Islam, 43
Kazakhstan, 59
KGB, 6, 18, 19, 27, 36, 37,
    38, 39, 43, 46
    Latvian, 7
Kirov, Sergei, 42
Kohl, Helmut, 12
Kravchuk, Leonid, 43
Kremlin, 5, 7, 16, 20, 37, 60
    corruption in, 30
Kryuchkov, Vladimir, 6, 19,
    24, 26, 27, 32, 36
Khrushchev, Nikita, 36, 42

Landsbergis, Vitautas, 43, 51
Laptev, Ivan, 22
Lenin, Vladimir, 29, 31, 36,
    38, 42, 44
Leningrad, 8
Lukin, Vladimir, 18
Lukyanov, Anatoly, 39

Major, John, 12, 19
Marx, Karl, 42
Mensheviks, 42
Minsk, 60
Mitterrand, François, 12
Moiseyev, Mikhail, 19, 32, 39
Moscow News, 6
Moscow Radio, 19

NKVD (see KGB)
Nicolas, Czar, 42
Nixon, Richard, 55

Pavlov, Valentin, 6, 7, 19, 22
Perestroika, 20, 33, 36, 41, 42, 60
  definition of, 6
Pogroms, 11
Politburo, 41
Pravda, 16, 44
Pugo, Boris, 7, 32
Pyankov, Boris, 32

Radio Russia, 6
Reagan, Ronald, 55
Red Square, 5, 16, 37
Russian Federation Building (*see* Russian Parliament)
Russian Parliament, 8, 10, 13, 16, 17, 18, 20, 21, 22, 23, 24, 34, 39, 40, 45, 59
Russian Social-Democratic Labor Party, 42
Russian Television, 6
Russian "White House," (*see* Russian Parliament)

St. Basil's Cathedral, 5
SALT treaty, 55
Shaposhnikov, Yevgeny, 39, 52, 53
Shebarshin, Leonid, 32, 39

Shevardnadze, Eduard, 18, 37
Siberia, 18
Simes, Dimitri, 59
Soviet Republics
  Council of the Republics, 51
  Council of Union, 51
  independence of, 48
  Inter-Republican Economic Committee, 52
Soviet Union
  nuclear arsenal, 56
  withdrawal from Afghanistan and Cuba, 57
Starodubsev, Vasil, 7
Stalin, Joseph, 19, 31, 36, 42, 46
START treaty, 57
State Committee for the State of Emergency, 5, 6, 8, 10, 12, 19, 22
Stavropol, 49
Supreme Soviet, 13, 42, 52
Sverdlov, Yakov, 38

Tiananmen Square, 16
Tizyakov, Aleksandr, 7, 24, 26
Trushin, Vasily, 32

Ukraine, 43, 44, 46
United Nations, 52

United States
  foreign policy, 55

Voice of America, 11, 13

Walesa, Lech, 11
World War II, 55

Yanayev, Gennady, 5, 6, 11, 12, 13, 14, 19, 21, 22, 34
Yazov, Dmitri, 6, 19, 20, 24, 26, 32, 39
Yeltsin, Boris
  allegiance to, 15, 20, 24, 26, 35, 41
  career of, 33
  leadership role after coup failure, 43, 44, 60
  and Mikhail Gorbachev, 17, 26, 34, 39, 40, 51, 52, 59
  opposition to coup attempt, 8, 10, 18, 19–22
  opposition to Gorbachev, 30, 49
  resignation from Communist party, 33, 42
  support from U.S., 17, 56
  threats from hardliners, 12
Yeremey, Grigory, 43